Gone But Not Forgotten

PHOTO POEMS BY O. JAMES FOX

INTRODUCTION BY WILMA L. GIBBS

LAWRENCEBURG PUBLIC LIBRARY

Provided
through the generosity of
Indianapolis Power & Light Company
Indiana Historical Society Press

D1209147

INDIANA HISTORICAL SOCIETY INDIANAPOLIS 2000

1
305.896097
FOX

A young Jim Fox, 1945

MAR   2004

Introduction

It always amazes me when people and events in my life come full circle. When I started work at the Indiana Historical Society as program archivist for African American history, I arrived at the completion of a collecting venture called the Black Women in the Middle West Project. The Society, along with four other repositories in Illinois and Indiana, cooperated to identify, collect, and archive manuscript and photographic collections pertaining to black women. Historian Darlene Clark Hine directed the project, which also included the Chicago Historical Society, the Illinois State Historical Library, the Calumet Regional Archives, and the Northern Indiana Historical Society. In February 1987 the *New York Times* published an article about the project, and several newspapers throughout the country picked up the wire service story. Ohioan O. James Fox, who had worked in Indianapolis as a photographer and display technician for Flanner House, a social service agency created in 1898 to ease the assimilation of a migrant, rural population adjusting to a northern city, read the story in the *Cleveland Plain Dealer*. Afterwards, he wrote to the Society, offering many of the negatives and photographs that he had taken while he lived in Indianapolis. Most of the images were dated from 1945 to 1960. More recently, inspired by the Society's move to its new building located on the Central Canal in downtown Indianapolis, Fox shared a group of photographs and poems from an earlier exhibition in Ohio entitled *The Canal*. Many of those items are contained within this exhibition catalog.

I remember O. James Fox. I recall the tall, lanky white man who took pictures in our Indianapolis neighborhood when I was a small child growing up on the near west side. Everyone knew Fox. He used his Rollei to photograph neighborhood buildings, scenes, and families, especially children. He started a camera club for young people that met at the Morgan Health Center, a building adjacent to Flanner House. Although I have not seen the image since I was a child, I remember the photograph he took of my brother over forty years ago. The photograph had a shadow and illuminated a four-year-old boy dressed in short pants, with a tear-stained face. The picture was taken on the north side of West Fifteenth Street in front of the Health Center—where we faithfully got vaccinations for polio and tuberculosis.

O. James Fox came to Indianapolis in 1945, after volunteering for overseas duty with the American Friends Service Committee (AFSC). The AFSC assigned the Ohioan to an urban work camp in Indianapolis. The camp was part of Flanner House, which was located on the near west side. It engaged its neighbors, as well as other citizens, in a wide range of programs that were running at full throttle. Flanner House offered child care, recreation, crafts, food preparation, sewing, and the building trades. It provided practical training in several areas.

When Fox came to Indianapolis, one of his first jobs was to photodocument the slum area on the near west side of the city. The slum clearance project opened up much-needed land for returning soldiers and their families. Flanner House spearheaded a major self-help project that built houses for individuals who were willing to contribute sweat equity. Most of those homes remain in the possession of the families that built them.

The neighborhood had large grasshoppers, praying mantises, and ladybugs, which we temporarily captured in ventilated glass jars. There were also tulips, dandelions, peonies, roses, and huge sunflowers in the summertime. Gliders and swings furnished most porches. We played hide-and-seek, foursquare, and hopscotch and jumped rope underneath the big cigar tree. "Mother May I" was a favorite. Like the flower Sharon and the star Hitsie that Fox photographed, we exuded all the innocence and beauty that childhood projects. We played in the streets and alleys, in our yards, and at Flanner House. Although we were the neighborhood children and did not generally mix, except at school, with the children whose parents paid for their child care, the Flanner House staff treated us the same. We climbed the monkey bars and played on the slides and swings, played sports with all the competitive gusto that we could muster, and indulged in crafts.

On cold, snowy, or rainy days, we stayed inside and drank hot chocolate, read library books, and watched westerns in the morning and the *Little Rascals* in the afternoon. We played board games such as Monopoly (although we preferred Finance), and our competitive spirits soared whenever we played Scrabble and Password. When we went outside we made snowmen and jumped through mounds of snow.

Within three blocks of my house on the same street, there were at least five churches, and two of them were Baptist. Down the street was Charles Sumner School No. 23, where black teachers nurtured black children. Mr. Harry's, a family grocery store, was around the corner on Fourteenth Street, next to the tavern.

It was a very structured environment. There were mental boundaries that kept young children within a two-block radius. And there were the physical barriers that helped make the neighborhood a self-contained cocoon. One such barrier was the Canal—most of the neighborhood people crossed it at Twelfth or Fifteenth Streets. When we made the sojourn from Missouri Street to Crispus Attucks High School to the west, we trekked across the Twelfth Street Bridge. And many afternoons we walked east, crossed the railroad tracks, and went to Central Library. The great divide—Sixteenth Street—sprawled directly to the north. It was a very busy, well-traveled boulevard. I knew if one ventured far enough west in May, zooming race cars would be swirling nonstop around an oval track. My family experienced the 500-Mile Race every year, conjuring up the greatest spectacle in racing through our collective mind's eye, as we sat in the backyard amid the smell of holiday barbecue and listened to it on the radio.

The neighborhood was deluged with all the sounds, smells, and sights of the urban landscape. Fox captured many of the latter. He photographed stark images of conditions along the Central Canal. Dilapidated structures, outdoor pumps, and trash contrasted to children fishing and a centenarian growing old gracefully. His photography and his poetry describe the houses on Mill, Missouri, Twelfth, and West Streets. In 1956 he took color photographs of street scenes of Indiana Avenue stretching from downtown to Tenth Street. Many of these photographs are contained in the O. James Fox Collection (P 266) at the Society. He writes about, and his poems capture, many aspects of Indiana Avenue—a jazz venue that was in its heyday from the 1930s through the 1960s. His visual images and poetry for the western edge of the community include parades, entrepreneurial endeavors, nightlife, emergency runs, and buildings.

With his poems and photographs, O. James Fox poignantly depicts what he saw as he served as an eyewitness to one neighborhood in Indianapolis during the post–World War II period. Although urban renewal and an interstate belt have altered and demolished the physical structures, Fox's work bears witness to an era and a community.

Wilma L. Gibbs
Program Archivist

Photo of Mr. Jim taken by a camera club member

now that time has had its say

Time the runner has swiftly passed us by.
We wonder if the water still flows
Through the City.

We've heard it doesn't,
That now on super highways
Automobiles dash in and out,
Taking up the water course.

Some historical archaeologists
Can probably discern why the Canal was built,
From where it took its water
And where it flowed,
of what use it was.

We knew it started out north.
We walked the path alongside
That horses toiled to draw the boats.

We thought that the quiet stream
Could have use for canoes and parasols
Like a painting by Degas.

Of course such dreams came to naught.
The city planners had to accommodate
The gas burners.

Since I stayed near the Canal for many years,
I thought it took on a spiritual meaning.
Now that Time has had its say,
I wonder if anyone else remembers.

children's party

They came to show the Quaker way,
How friends could cross old lines
Drawn in some other day.

They lived and worked in this old place,
Cleaned things up with cheerful smiles,
Talked to neighbors of the other race.

The girls one day thought the time had come
To invite the children for a garden party.
By doing this, some hearts would be won.

The children came with quiet dreams,
Played the games with happy skill,
Then joined the circle to eat ice cream.

By one way to look, they were deprived,
But they weren't strangers to festive fun.
In church and school things were more alive.

What held their interest was another thing.
In the souls of the girls was friendly love.
That's what made the drab day sing.

Among the girls there was especially one.
Her saintly visage earned place in every thought.
The way she moved to lift each child's soul;
Their hearts she won, life's threads caught.

a flower grows on missouri street

This summer is passing on time's fleet wings.
The macadam gets too hot for bare feet and
The heat of gardens rises in columns of the sun.

In children's minds, the mirages shimmer
From the heated earth.
Along Missouri Street, it's easy to hope,
To believe,
To soar like birds.

This may be a rickety slum sinking into the rubble,
But somehow this flower grows.
Her name is Sharon.

star reaching

No one knows what Hitsie sees.
This happy concentration is not yet dulled.
Amused, retained, transfixed in some eternal moment.
Her complex mind reaches back through dark nights.
Here she is, another chance, no one knows
What her mind sees, what she will become.
Now she's reaching, looking up.

106th Summer

She wore a dark, full length dress with polka dots
And often had her pet chicken on her lap
To excite the picture taker's interest.

I wasn't much for learning all the details about a person,
But I did find out that she was from New Orleans,
Originally.

She was over the hundred year mark and didn't figure
That she was a part of the environment in which
She found herself.

She was an odd and lonely inhabitant along the Canal.
Her shack stood not five feet off 12th Street.
Inside she had a neat brass bed and an ironing board,
A wood stove, and a place to prepare food,
No electricity.

Her place was very clean, seemed white-washed inside,
Only one room, a ceramic pot behind her bed.

She looked forward to my traverses of the Bridge.
I never failed to draw up from my swooping glides.
One day, though, she was no longer there.

Her neighbors were very proud that
She had just had her 106th birthday.

some things are better left unsaid

I've often wondered about this.
There are things one shouldn't write about,
Some things almost impossible to photograph.
Some I did, most I didn't.

How about the boy we tried to give a job?
One night he climbed a back alley fence
And was shot by the police.

And the boy who carried an ice pick
And was known to have used it.

The pretty brown skin girl
Who started working Senate Avenue
At fourteen

The summer night when we all gathered
On 14th Street near Senate
When sirens wailed;
A crazed husband had ambushed two policemen
With shotgun blasts.

I wasn't from the ash-can photo school
I wanted to show the dignity people projected,
The happy play and friendly gatherings.

We had to show the dilapidated structures,
the outdoor pumps, the ragged clothes.
But some other theme insisted on our attention,
Startling beauty, quiet serenity,
Unspoken determination.

The Canal flowed quietly after the rigors
Of winter.
It talked to us, a better day was coming.

A small child looked up at my Rollei lens.
God placed beauty in the most unlikely places.

the avenue as a magician

On a summer night, the Canal reflected bright lights
In neon flares and wiggles.

The water coursed under the Avenue running diagonally,
And the Canal was mysteriously lost to view.

The Avenue had its own life
In slanting opposition to the sacred river.

In the light of day, the Avenue showed
Its gray reality of decrepit fronts.

In the waning light, a parade went by,
The uniformed marchers in practiced unison,
Drew stares from curb and windows.
On another day, a spectacle motorcade pushed back reality.
General Ike, under whom many had served,
Was running for President.

Then, Sunset drew other crowds,
To watch the arrival of Diz, the trumpeter.
From a long, stretch limo, his entourage had alighted,
To tune the brass and balance up the sound equipment.

As night descended, neon mystery made sensate illusion
And phantom dreams that lured the dispossessed.

Cars cruised slowly down the Avenue,
As a summer storm wet the street
And mirrored the flow of colors.

At the other end, near downtown, a favorite bar, Henri's
Dispensed scotch and water in the dim haze of smoke and light
And set a stage for the local jazz musicians.

Back in the dim dark on a transluscent sheen, the Canal still flowed,
Its surface rippled with the falling rain.

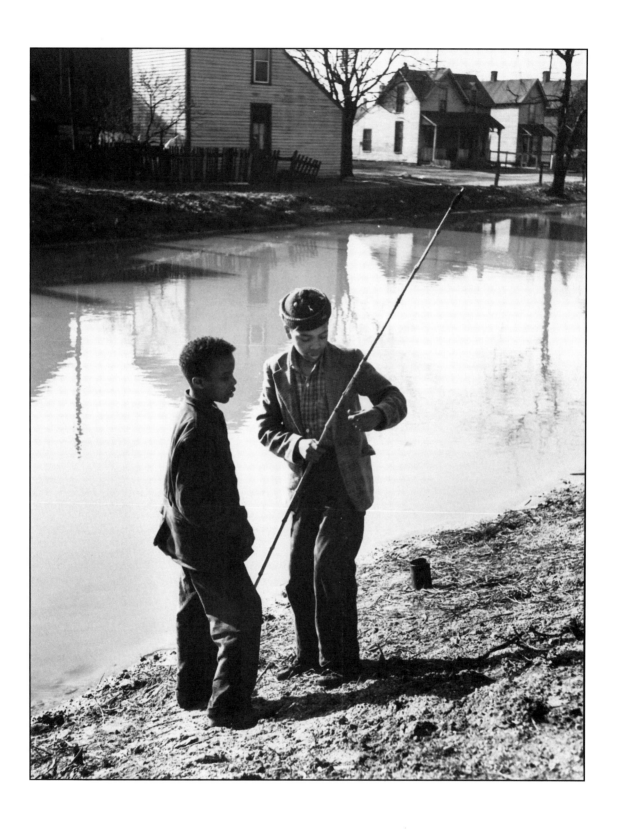

view from a bicycle

I saw the Canal running placidly through the city.
Leaves floated gracefully, slowly turning.
People threw garbage into it.
Flotsam drifted like little boats set afloat.

The mirror it proposed was dreamlike.
It reflected the squalor, but also the boys playing.
Upon the silver water, people were crossing bridges,
A spiritual illusion.

The 12th Street crossing had a curving lift.
My bicycle went up and over in a swooping glide.
I glanced out over the silver sheen
To see what was being reflected.
It told stories about nature and the decrepit
Place through which it flowed.
One could imagine the deprived people along its bank
Were benefitting from the spiritual message of the Canal.

Its peaceful imitation of decay, junk, machinery, and trees,
Altered reality.
The shimmering etchings gave some joyful lift
And encouraged those who traversed its banks.
It painted changing pictures more artfully than any painter.
It tinted the edges of degradation with romantic illusion.

At night, the reflection of lights was awesome.
Standing on the 12th Street bridge
With the girl I loved, we gazed in wonder.
Our ship was at sea
And beyond was a starlit ocean.

spring will come

When spring would trip in one day on balmy winds,
Wearing garlands of green leaves and flowers,
The young men would start returning,
Not in a rush, but quietly,
To the arms of families they had once known.

Many packed .45 automatics against muscular flanks,
Sported an aggressiveness, an elan,
Foreign to the quiet eddies,
They left long ago.

That return was still to come.
In this smoky Indian summer,
The people of these dusty streets
Were unconsciously struggling,
Quietly nurturing,
Caring for the children,
Preserving happy spirits the best they could,
Shielding the embers of their dreams.

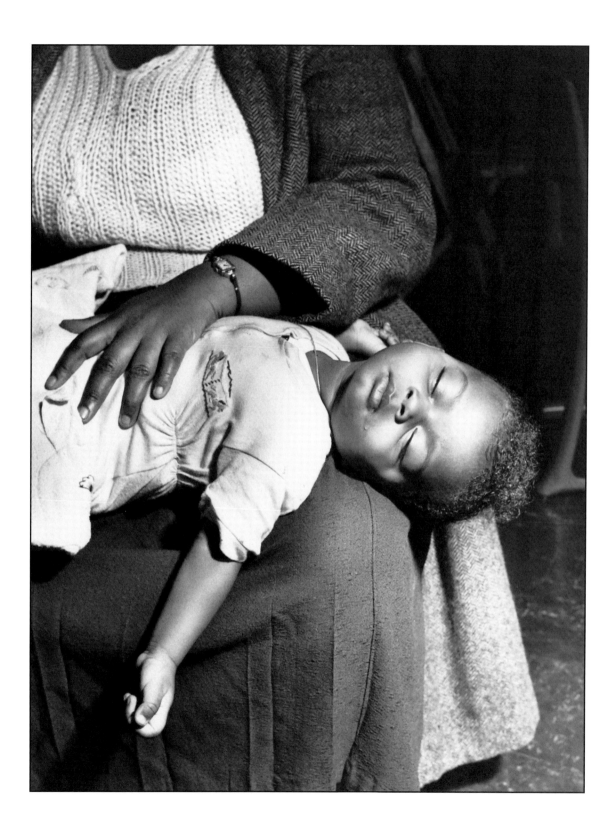

everyone has a story

The 12th Street bridge made a crossover
From North West and Mill Streets
To Missouri Street.

On Mill Street were neat one-story houses
With picket fences around the yards.
On 12th Street were low one-story shacks.
On Missouri Street were odd two-story dwellings,
Weathered green or gray, flaking intricacies
Of old paint.

Behind these strange, peaked facades
Lay mystery.
Who were these people?

From some homes, strange odors emanated, greasy smells,
Aromatic driftings on the humid air.

I was a strange, fleeting figure with a smile,
my Rollei slung over one shoulder—
Its vertical, double eyes staring
With glassy objectivity.
My eyes were hooded, never showing aversion
Or censorship.
Yet I was not indeterminate.
I was part of it, fragile, pursued by my own
Adversities, my bad foot, vague governmental
Propensities,
When revealed in my eyes, like theirs.

Yet, I didn't exhibit self-pity.
I seemed to flaunt a lucky look to people
who bought their tickets for the numbers
Every day.

The old lady with the pure white chicken
Noticed it.
Curious, she became interested, dressed up
And fixed her hair, in anticipation
Of my regular run by her shack.

another day, another people

In the days when the Great War was grinding to a halt,
In the heartland of America,
Far from the crash of bombs
And the rattle of machine gun fire,
The life of the city ebbed and flowed.

Children played along the Canal and on the back streets.
Old men plodded with pushcarts through the alleys.
Along the avenues, the houses looked like wrecks of ships
Whose sea flights had ended.
Women cooked and washed.
Pungent, greasy smells floated from open doors.

Summer raised the hot dust,
Crushed the people in its warm, expansive arms.
Children fished for crayfish in the Canal.
Youth strolled past the derelict backgrounds
And played ball.

Late summer days crept by in soft, smoky sunlight.
Crisp, white frost greeted the early workers
One morning,
On their ways to hotels, restaurants, factories,
And downtown buildings;
The children on the skip and run for school.

In the natural cycle of seasons, winter gripped the city
And drove inhabitants indoors to the warmth
Of coal furnaces and red hot oil stoves in drafty rooms.

Soon, coal dust permeated the air outdoors.
The drab weariness of cold winter emphasized the lonely separations.
In the quiet, gray days and black nights, unspoken worry reached
Across oceans
To soldiers enduring combat in wintry forests,
To sailors on icy decks.

winter time wonders

One winter night after being in the City
For several months,
We decided to go out north
Of 38th Street,
To have a friendly snowball fight.
Getting out of the car,
We asked each other,
"What's that odd smell?"
After a number of sniffs,
Billie exclaimed,
"Why that's fresh air!"

Asked to a house
Where I had agreed to loan the family
Ten dollars,
Stepped out of the car into drifts
Of snow and ten degree cold,
Was assailed at the door
With blast furnace heat.
The oil stove was red hot
And the stove pipe was aglow.
There were four children
In the shadows
And a baby.
The fumes from the oil stove
Permeated the heated air
From table top to ceiling.
It was cold on the floor.

tips for night riders

When you turn away from the streets
Running near the Canal,
Where church-going folks are sleeping,
Or caring for their children,
After the curfew, streets seem deserted.

The dark night closes in
With roulette dangers.
Lights are beckoning on the Avenue,
Sending out their neon signals.

Keep doors locked and windows up.
Maintain speed, but not too fast.
That car that's swerving,
Give him room.

Look back to see who follows.
Turn right, see what happens.
Think of the shortest route
To the nearest precinct station.

That car that's stopped
In the middle of the intersection,
Shattered glass,
And steaming radiator.

A man collapsed from
the door swung open,
Bleeding forehead and glassy eyes,
Raised fingers in a disconnected gesture.

Don't stop!
Don't help him, bleeding,
Into your clean car!
Don't make the run to General Hospital!
Don't talk and yell to keep him conscious!
Don't speed up to the emergency entrance
And shout for help,
This man is dying!

I want to be loved

From the roof the speakers vibrated with sound waves,
Rocked and resonated in the dancers below.

Paper lanterns brought romance to the dusty macadam,
Reflected in the eyes of dancers, whirling
To the shuffling beat.

The darkness of the summer night made infinite walls
For our outdoor ballroom.

The words of songs formed on upturned lips,
I want to be loved until the dawning,
I want to be loved only by you.

The entire neighborhood from little jitterbugs
To oldsters on canes,
Were transformed by rhythmic
And distant dreams.

Then on the scene
Swaggered four young men
From way across town.

They chose the prettiest young girls,
Danced and whirled;
The others gave way
To stand and watch.

Soon sirens wailed,
The record scratched and stopped,
The young men whose girls were lost
Had charged in to fight to defend their turf.

The crowd dispersed, the lights were out.
From dreams emerged
The drab, gray street
We knew.

free enterprise cafe

Invited to a night life feature of the neighborhood,
I brought my camera with its flashing bulbs.
In this case, however, the Rollei lens
Was not to be uncapped.
The hostess merely thought I might
Enjoy myself one Saturday night.

I wondered at the scene
As several couples sat at tables in the cleaned up room.
From the kitchen, women peered expectantly;
On the menu, hamburgers and fries, chitlins, or ribs.

One could also order whiskey straight
Or in a Coca Cola.
Later in the quiet scene, cards were played.

As midnight chimed, legal green was shown
As checks were professionally tendered,
And change was made with clinking coins.

On this decorous occasion, in this simple place,
Unlicensed, free enterprise was blooming.

LAWRENCEBURG PUBLIC LIBRARY
123 WEST HIGH ST.
LAWRENCEBURG, IN 47025